A Message From Source

Beautiful and inspiring
poetry of the spirit

Grace Gabriella Puskas

WINNER OF THE LOCAL LEGEND
SPIRITUAL WRITING COMPETITION

A record of this publication is available from the British Library.

ISBN 978-1-910027-00-4

Typesetting by Wordzworth Ltd
www.wordzworth.com

Cover design by Titanium Design Ltd
www.titaniumdesign.co.uk

Printed by Lightning Source UK
www.lightningsource.com

Cover image © Caitlin Bracken

Illustrations © Aleksandra Grzebalska

LOCAL LEGEND

Published by Local Legend
www.local-legend.co.uk

Dedication

This book is dedicated to life itself and to all of the beings and experiences that have shaped my journey. I also give my love and thanks to my mother, without whom this would not have been possible due to the endless support and love she has shown.

Acknowledgements

The illustrations have been generously given by Aleksandra Grzebalska, in a beautiful example of life's synchronicity and of how connected we are when we awaken to our purpose. Aleksandra's creativity was inspired by her attunement to Reiki by the author.

am.grzebalska@gmail.com

The Gift Is Life Itself has been kindly donated by Susanne Austin, a writer, presenter, mentor and guide for personal and planetary wellbeing.

info@susanneaustin.co.uk

Caitlin Bracken, visionary artist and intuitive co-creator at *The Cosmic Butterfly*, has designed the beautiful front cover in exchange for Reiki healing and attunement to the Reiki healing system.

caitlinb.design@gmail.com

About This Book

Every so often, though rarely, a very special new voice is heard in the world. It does not shout. It does not need to use pompous phrases or bad language to get your attention. Indeed, at first, you may not even realise that it has spoken to you. But once its words have entered your mind, they reach deep within your consciousness. And you are changed, your outlook on life different.

This collection is such a voice. It is the debut book of an exceptionally talented young author, destined to be a major influence in the fields of consciousness and spirituality. She writes thoughtfully and with focus, in language with which we are all familiar. Even if you might not normally choose to read poetry, allow these words to flow through you - even speak them aloud - and they will inspire you on a path of awakening to higher states of awareness, spiritual connection and love.

Grace explores the power of meditation, the nature of the universe and of time, our connection to the environment, our subjective perception and who we are as creative beings of light and sound.

WINNER OF THE NATIONAL LOCAL LEGEND
SPIRITUAL WRITING COMPETITION

About The Author

Although in her early twenties, Grace Puskas is a qualified Reiki Master, crystal healer and herbalist, in addition to being experienced in meditation, sound healing and shamanic healing. She has travelled widely, spending time in Buddhist centres and volunteering on conservation and organic farming projects in Thailand and Malaysia. A selection of her poetry performances called *How to Live in Bliss Through a Magical Journey of Language* is available at *www.source.tv*, an online platform for spiritual teachers, healers and light workers to share knowledge.

www.gracepuskas.moonfruit.com

Contents

This is a journey of Grace,
a story from the sounds of space
of the timeless time that creates...
Voice these words aloud to yourself.
Allow the words on the page to recreate the dream
and travel through the realms of mind, unknown, unseen...

Soul Sisters

Shadow Surfacing

Twin Flame

Ancient Lovers

Perceived Point Of View

Soul Seduction

A Journey Through Grace

The Peace Within

Star Seed Secrets

Dream Space Dreamers

Mother's Creation

Child's Play

Once Upon A Time

A Mermaid's Tale

Galactic Time Traveller

The Gift Is Life Itself

Sound Synapse

Would You?

Would you fear me
if I told you I could read your mind
and count you into the room on time?
Would you fear me
if I could get inside your head,
know your fears, your doubts and inner pain,
if I were to say that this is a game
that I've already won but you're playing my way?
If I were to say I could control your actions
as I powerfully create through love and compassion,
would you fear me?

Would you fear me
if I knew what to say at the perfect time,
if I could breathe through your being and heal your mind
by looking directly into your eyes?
If I could uplift your spirit purely through eye contact,
if I could hold my hand to your heart and help you feel
    love,
if you could feel the energy travel through the air
as it came from my hands with a magical flare?
If you could feel the healing and know from where it
    came,
would you realise your own power - or create lies and
    pain?

1

Would you accuse me of lying if I said I could feel your
    inner truth,
see behind the surface and bring out the true you?
Would you doubt me, deny me, or make me seem crazy,
would you argue, withdraw, accuse me or hate me?
Would you hate me
if I always seemed undisturbed
by your ego, judgement or unnecessary harsh words?
Or if you were to fail despite all your intention
to decrease my energy and inhibit my momentum,
would you avoid me?

Would you avoid me
if I were to try and raise your vibration,
if I were to try and expand your mind by asking more
    questions?
Or if I were to offer you healing through speech,
to try and tell you that words can physically heal your
    body,
would you avoid me?
If I were to say that I know when you lie,
and I know your desires and can see through your smile,
if I were to say I see deep within your soul and the
    suffering you hide,
would you allow me to help you?

Would you allow me to help you
if I were to say I can get straight to the root
and take on your pain as if I were you?
If I told you I know the cause of your fear and how to
    transcend it,
would you fear me or allow me to help you, my friend?

If I were to say that everything is vibration,
if I were to tell you I could heal your own tension
by unblocking your chakras through love and intention,
would you fear me?
If I could visualise light around your third eye
and change your thought processes in that instant of
    time,
would you believe me?

Would you believe me
if I said I exist on a frequency of light,
of magic and healing and infinite supply?
If I were to say the universe is my playground,
and I am the creator who allows the Earth to spin round,
would you believe me?
If I were to tell you I've learned the secrets of life's game,
reached the top, came back to help, and chosen the
    middle way,
or if I were to say I am Christ consciousness incarnate,
and the only reason I am here is to help transcend pain,
would you love me?

Would you love me
if I were to say I've felt the whole Earth's suffering,
I've transcended the karmas to help us evolve
and I've come from the future to bring us all home,
would you love me?
If I were to tell you every day when I awake
I wish for universal harmony, peace and no hate,
or if I were to say that my true desire is love,
and if granted one wish it would truly be selfless,
would you love me?

If I told you this body was a channel for Source,
and this mind you perceive is a reflection of yours,
or if I were to say I am here solely for you
and I exist as a mirror to help you find truth,
would you love me?
What if I were to say that this is your dream
and I am here as your guide to allow you to be...?

Now, if I were to say every word is a lie
and it's all an illusion created by mind,
would you care?
Would it matter if these words had never been spoken?
Would it change your life to know that this path would
    have always been chosen?
Would you love me or hate me, fear me or all three?
What if I were to say that the only truth is what you
    believe...?

I Am

I am a tree...
I can feel you, but you choose not to feel me.
I give you life, yet you choose not to breathe.
I am a mighty tree...
sustaining all that is through my leaves,
through the roots that ground me and the air that we
    breathe,
through the invisible energy that connects you and me.
I am a powerful tree...
My trunk supports,
sustaining our life force.
Yet do you see me? Feel me? Do you even believe me?
Why would you care if I cannot be measured by money?

I am an eternal tree...
I exist with this Earth for as long as there is sea,
I am alive for long after all the animals decease.
I am appreciated by all such as the birds and the bees,
as they realise to survive they must live in harmony with
    me.
They give back what they take through the balance of life.
They allow for the natural laws of universal supply.

I am an infinite tree...
with endless possibilities for creation and growth.

In the beginning I was one and this one was the Word.
The Word or the Earth or the sea or the breeze...
language takes all away from the feelings I see,
and I feel how your human mind likes to perceive,
to break things into pieces and destroy and deceive.
If only you realised how connected you are to me,
then you might truly see
that you are a tree...

Human Angel

I am a human angel,
my emotions creating the personality of form,
the disguise of persona forming this formless avatar;
a humane angle
of shapes and vibrations,
geometric sounds of persuasion.

Words flow through these channels in metaphor,
energy zones connecting cosmic corridors
through consciousness, to these meridians that electrify,
electrical frequencies conscious of the power to intensify,
to change the dream,
create the unseen,
see the creation,
live through manifestation,
and manifest through dreaming the change.

The humane angles that make up this angel
contain memories stored in the structure of DNA,
our spiral of remembering strands consumed by
    darkness,
once lost to the game
of forgetting how to be human,
by loving, ascending and recognising what it means to be
    human.

Re-cognising mind and body with spirit
that swims into the existence of this physical adaptation,
experiencing higher realms and dimensions,
being open to the frequencies of light and surprising
    sensations,
living through the sound and silence of geometric
    vibration,
adapting to exist in this infinite ocean of word,
thought, action and rhyme,
creating the paradox of the illusion of time.

And when I am unattached from the ego's thought forms
    and speech,
I can fully spread my wings,
flying free from this three-dimensional reality.

Our Story

This is my story.
This is your story.
This is our planet's story.
This is the universe's story.
This is a story of time and space.
This is a story of truth.
Yet what is truth
but a story?

This is a fairy tale.
This is fiction.
This is the greatest love story ever told.
This is a factual depiction.
This story makes perfect sense.
This story brings confusion.
This is the truth of all life's questions.
Yet this story is still
an illusion.

A Message From Source

The power is coming,
the ego is running,
desperate in pursuit,
departure right in view.
Hand, heart and eye are becoming more in time
with the rhythm of the music;
yet in my darkest hour, time and tide
wait for no man or goddess in this rollercoaster ride.
Ups and downs, smiles and frowns, wrong or right,
yet does it matter if I always have my sight,
this higher eye that takes me deep into the night of this
    fight or flight,
and magical delight?
Round and round in this repetitive recording I spin
until my crown once more becomes in sync
with the roots that ground me,
the true self, waiting patiently.

Feet are flooded by the waters of vibration,
giving life to my tree of salvation.
Whilst sun and moon offer their support,
it's only up to me to open up my door
and surrender to the love and let the light come shining
    in,
allowing the prophesised song to sing, and win.

More than any heart or soul could ask for,
yet exactly what I shall provide, and more.
As soon as time allows, my mind succumbs to the
    emptiness of centre,
re-energising my being with water that remembers
exactly who I am and the reason I was sent here.
For some I am yet another marching in obedient line,
yet in my world I am the creator, pure nature,
source anxiously at ease,
swirling through the breeze until all that is becomes one
    with this body,
this temple of bliss healing slowly but surely.

Disease of thought tries to pollute my river
while destiny of dream sends me signs that deliver
true insight and meaning, within the reality that deceives
    my face of wisdom.
Yet dreams have been showing that my true essence
is growing back to the one sound of compassion.
This comes only from within,
yet simultaneously I swim through rhythmic currents on
    the outside of this skin;
no difference between inner and outer,
me as the centre being the point of divine mergence.
For the spirit and form go hand in hand,
a balance essential to stay connected to our homeland.

The yin and the yang... the woman and man...
the spirit and form... the calm breeze and storm.
Wrong and right... fear and flight... dark and light.
Seed to tree or tree to seed... roots to crown or the other
    way round.

Thinking and feeling... destruction and healing.
Thought and no mind... time/space and space/time...
    divine and animal mind.
Now and eternal... inner, external...
knowing, believing... creating and receiving.
King and queen and god and goddess, conscious,
or unconsciously marching along like ants and robots.
Bad and good... drought and flood...
rush and slow wave... life is a game
between the sound and the silence;
so we all need reminding of the balance required to live
    life in harmony,
all dualistic natures existing in a state of non-duality,
    merging as unity.
Ego and self not separate but one;
one consciousness distorted through the singing of life's
    song.

Yet what life has shown me throughout this timeless dream,
is that inner to outer is the only way to live life in balance.
The elements of nature being the core of our essence
more connected to Source, providing a permanent sense
    of security
and freedom from fear,
blissfully riding the wave of existence.
For there is more to the senses than the average eye
    sees;
instinct and intuition allow us to flow through our
    unfolding destiny,
never missing a moment of magic or helping opportunity.
For when we are completely content, with no attachments
    or fears,

this is all we wish for:
for every sentient soul to be free from their mind-created
    sufferings
and realise their true power, and more.

Like a bright star wandering through the spaces...
like a peacefully at ease tree with many enlightening
    faces...
like a drop of unpolluted water floating slowly down life's
    stream...
like a fully charged atom connected to the air we breathe,
    to everything,
to you and me, sun and sea, air and tree...
In this state of being every moment is a blessing,
not desiring anything for our being so that everything we
    are receiving
is a free gift from life,
allowing us to view others without afflictive emotion
and feel genuine joy from their delight,
with selfless sight.
When looking into another's eyes, we see them for who
    they are,
their core, their essence of pure light
and only have compassion.
We feel their being,
use senses outside of the reality others are deceived in.
This is how to recreate perception;
with these eyes we realise they are a complete reflection
of us and our own nature, which is beauty and perfection.

Living life as a unity,
feeling your mirror's being, state of mind,

emotions, truth or lies,
reading them like a book as if you were the narrator,
sharing the same heartbeat, allowing you to create
joy and light, smiles and no fear or judgment
as the pretence of separation on all levels has been let
    go.
The spaces between you and others acting as synapses,
connecting you and them within a telepathic sea with no
    gaps,
allowing you to uplift and enlighten like a gift from above,
thereby continuing to feel blissful and attract situations of
    love.
With those who are hostile or judge and abuse your
    kindness,
you simply have compassion and remain in your inner
    stillness.

This state of being which all religions promise will save us,
the goddesses and gods that are innate within each one of
    us,
or the Buddha who achieved enlightenment by oneness
    with a tree;
this has always been, throughout space and time, you
    and me.
The kundalini and chakras - or whichever words language
    chooses -
the extra-terrestrials, the Buddha or the shamans,
the light beings, witches or the angels,
the eternal beings, healers or the aliens...
these are just words for our higher nature,
the state of consciousness and awareness we can live life
    in forever more.

We are the rainbow generation,
the light split into colour due to the physicality of
    observation,
the one harmonious sound being distorted through
    differing notes.
Musical rhythms in a magical dance,
awakening from our repetitive trance
that the imbalance has created
throughout all patterns and ages.
A snap-shot within a snap-shot, above to below,
universal cycles reflecting in the world we think we know.
So if we choose to get in tune with what is occurring on a
    cosmic scale,
being the light that shines and seeing through the veil,
the world of magic... music... light...
the dancing heartbeat we call life
can be lived by us moment to moment,
enabling the planet we need and love to survive.

These words I have narrated are not a fictional fairy tale,
this is the new reality, the one conscious entity
if only we embrace our multi-dimensional reality.
So now the harmonious song of love and joy
is dancing back towards the light;
it is up to us as individuals to remain in fear and
    suffering
or choose to spread our wings and fly...
The I is just here for the ride.

A Love of Nothing

I am just human, after all.
I may be everything,
at one with every thing,
yet I am no thing.
And if these words were to disappear from this page,
or if I were to leave without a single trace,
would I be missed?
Would any of it make a difference?

As I allow these thoughts to take hold,
I can feel my essence fade away,
instantly feeling sadness, hurt and pain.
All I am is memory.
Empty.
And there really is no purpose.
Regardless of my beliefs - or truth - can I ever really be
    certain

of any thing?
Once again, I remind myself, I am no thing.

Now I think of all the people in my life
and if they know I'm feeling all alone and dead inside
and if they'd truly care...
With all the problems we create in our own lives,

would they really push aside their own despair?
The darkness just increases as the mind is thinking,
self-doubt and depression sink in....

How can we ever truly know the sacrifices others make?
How can we be aware of the energy others put into
making this world a better place?
No-one knows that every single day
I put on my game face,
forcing myself to be brave,
to try and be the best I can –

saving Grace.

And even as I feel all this
I know I shall receive resistance.
I know that there are many who will carelessly dismiss this
and the people whom I love and express this for
could choose to actively ignore
everything I stand for and all I teach.

So why do I still speak?

The single tear that's rolling down my face will say it all,
the pounding in my heart gives me determination not to fall,
the courage to continue with my dream,
the strength I need to be the best me I can be.

People say that mountains can be moved by faith;
moreover, I propose that our entire cosmos can be
    changed
by love.

It's love that allows me still to know,
love that allows my light to grow,
and love allows these words still to be written
and sink in.
It's love that helps insecurity and doubt to fade to black
while memories of the power of light and faith come
    flooding back.

So every time I feel there is no purpose
and feel myself becoming consumed by the dark,
I remind myself: yes - I am only human,
but a human with a heart.

The Meaning of Life

What is love?
Language cannot do this word justice
for love is a feeling,
the most powerful form of healing.

What is time?
Time is just a measurement,
a smell, a sound, a sight or touch,
to perceive an experience, a moment of love.

What is space?
Space allows everything to exist,
yet it is nothing, an eternal abyss.
Everything manifests from this empty void,
sounds, sights and matter being created and destroyed.

What is matter?
Matter is just the frequencies of sound
forming the physical world of sensations.
All matter is spiritual life force energies at different speeds,
our observing eyes creating the physical version
of what our mind perceives.

What is the meaning of life?
Now, breathe...
Close your eyes.

The Way of the Shaman

As I travel through these realms of energetic flow,
my mind merges with the Source, all tension letting go.
My psychic sense increases and I see colours, imagery
    and sacred geometry,
and sounds are sensed from a higher range of frequencies
as I communicate by telepathy.

My consciousness merges with all that is, experiencing
    the collective unconscious,
where archetypal ideas and insights into creation become
    integrated into the conscious.
My soul can freely travel to the inner worlds of light and
    connectivity,
where other beings become present, communication can
    occur,
and yet I still retain my sovereignty.

My heart grows and my mind expands, allowing guides
    and angels in,
yet I am always aware of my own power which comes
    directly from within.
By working with spirit and life force there's an increase in
    my healing ability;
I become a channel for power and raising awareness,
    rightfully accepting my divinity.

The way of the shaman is a dark light journey, taking on
  others' pain to heal;
with musical instruments and help from the plants, I
  allow myself truly to feel
the root of the pain and how to transcend, extracting disease from the soul's many bodies:
mental, emotional, physical, spiritual, all illness begins
  with anxieties.
Not separate from you, I can heal from the Source,
allowing your life to follow a different course.

My intent is to serve, be humble, to love, never judging
  but healing,
sharing with you a message of truth from the inner worlds
  of the mind;
from etheric realms, astral insights, time travelling
  wherever I find
I may access the unseen, receiving all knowledge and
  feeling.

Through the planes of the mind and dimensions of time,
  my soul exists in simultaneous realities.
I connect to the sky, the planets and stars, receiving
  wisdom from my lives in other galaxies.
Through the spiral of genetic connection, my awareness
  becomes conscious of lost memory.
I can feel the Earth's heartbeat, merge with nature's
  electromagnetic field, becoming a unified current of
  energy.

I talk to the plants, the crystals and animals, sharing
  their knowledge and loving intentions.

Dreamtime allows me to learn and receive, bringing
   healing power back for this dimension.
The most beautiful aspect of a shaman's story is
   surrender to the unknown and to all life's twists;
knowing this is a dream, imagined by mind, allows one to
   live in a state of pure bliss.

The Light in the Dark

The light in the dark, a realisation it takes us long to
    accept,
a denial of our true self we no longer can reject.
To mistake our identity and suppress our inner nature
is to judge others and their truth, prolonging spiritual
    venture.

The masculine and feminine desire to merge and nothing
    more,
a destiny written from the moment of our birth, and
    nature's law.
Within man lies his femininity, a caring and nurturing role;
within a woman lies assertiveness, essential to be whole.

Creation and destruction are the same point in time and
    space,
spirituality and sexuality two sides of the same face,
just like the serpent energy, the spiral that equates our
    spine;
disallowing this creative energy to flow suppresses the
    divine.

We judge or misconceive the dark aspects of our being,
because of oppression and suffering, the imbalance and
    unseeing.

The moon's energies are just as important for learning
    and for growth,
while absorbing only the sun's rays allows for
    destruction of our Earth.

We teach that the act of creation is wrong, harmful and a
    sin;
this destroys the very sacred essence that creates the skin
    we live in.
We deny the healing energies of moon and planets, and
    our own environment,
which results in us exerting a dominating role, focusing
    solely on one intent.

The left brain aspects are essential but only when
    combined with the right's,
when in harmony with each other we see that day flows
    into night.
From the night the sun arises and shines light upon our
    day,
which then cycles back to darkness in the eternal nature
    of life's game.

We must truly see the significance of balance and
    harmony,
fully accept the connected nature of spirituality, sexuality
    and creativity.
They are the three missing links, the same points in one
    circle;
by being the link, allowing this natural flow, we become a
    living miracle.

Moon Village

Cycling in the dark, no idea where I am going or which
    path to choose,
a bright light offers me vision and direction, with
    unwavering patience;
and now I follow this star child's shoes
to arrive in a community where everyone treats others all
    like family,
around a hypnotising fire, centring many beautiful
    energies
together in pure harmony.
These beings are simultaneously in constant dance,
some participating through connection with their
    instruments, forever thankful,
others flowing their bodies of perfection through the
    waves of every angle.
One with the air and in motion with the music,
not separate from the Source yet individual in how they
    fuse it.
This tribal gathering creating thunder, storm and
    lightning,
so many hands of power, fully aware of the strength of
    our energies combining.

I awake into a consciousness merged between worlds,
to feel a strong sensation of energy around my crown,

to see a swirling soul and hear a surreal sound,
a loud, mysterious breeze of wind wandering through the
    silence.
From the atmosphere experienced, reality perceived
    through altered timing,
I genuinely believe I have been visited by a spirit guide;
my thoughts derived from senses creating what's real by
    an observing eye,
this tai chi-ing being mistaken for a ghost by a deceiving
    mind.
Yet who can say what's real - it felt real in that moment -
and reality is just a mystery created by time, space and
    the mind;
so it matters not whether this soul was real, dead or alive,
as the magnitude of love travelled high into the night's skies.

Strangers freely dream in any location at will with no
    mention of any cost,
to be woken by a resident who smiles and says that
    moving to the fire would be more pleasant.
We are offered a feast of food, unlimited water and
    invitations to come and visit any time we choose.
I return, to be instantly reminded of just how united and
    unconditionally providing people can be,
offering food to many with no regards to money,
children growing up in natural scenery, the way it should be,
souls raising a family in a one-hearted community living
    by true hospitality.

So a message to the moon villagers...
May your life be forever filled with joy and laughter, peace
    and love,

and friendship with happy visitors.

May your positive energies the Earth eternally show,

and through your hearts help people learn and grow,

and enable the music never to cease its flow.

For everything, brothers and sisters... Domo arigato.

Mountain's Energy

Sitting on nature's rock in the middle of a jungle,
tail of waterfall flowing by my feet
while creatures so small circle breath's silent call.
Freedom is what is felt, free roam attained,
while a black and white butterfly flutters by my crown
    once more saved
by the splashing of water between both spaces of skin,
yet struggling against the stream as these spiders are
    showing disallows further swim.
From lines of connection from leaves to reflection's
    surface,
to patterns of geometry between breeze and trunks so
    earnest,
these eight-legged wanderers' homes create the timeless
    game,
the web of life re-living this new octave, in harmony once
    again.

Mystery man tells how the energy from the mountain
    differs by extreme
from the vibrations of sandy beaches, of island and of sea.
Yet the nameless soul's name matters not to the universal
    higher reality,
for what's real in the heart's eye, as this jungle shows, is
    true hospitality.

The ocean may provide the eye and beauty to see
how the waves connect sun, sea, tree, you and me;
yet crouching by mountain's stream with Mother Earth's
    urine trickling through my hand,
it's true that you can't take a poo in full view of Creation's
    mainland.

With Love, From You

Please listen to my message, listening is the key
from the silence created in meditation, allowing true
  harmony.
From my heart you truly are the perfection of nature's
  style -
a compassionate, caring and playful creature,
so humble with a lighting smile.

You always ask the perfect questions and know the right
  things to say
to help people find their truth, with your wise and patient
  ways.
Remember, my love, you will always be a wonderful
  inspiration;
and for this, and for how you learn and grow,
I offer all my appreciation.

You truly are pure light and love, so perfectly divine,
one person with whom I could willingly share all of my
  conscious time.
So thank you, my love, for sharing my journey throughout
  this eternal game;
you are a beautiful memory of truth and love,
and in heart and mind you will always remain.

Riddle of the Mind

Here is a riddle... what am I? Try to guess!
The most fertile of land I can make wilderness,
I pollute all your seas and break glass on your sands,
cause destruction to homes and burn down your lands,
I torture helpless animals to provide your disguise
with make-up and jewellery to misguide your true eyes.

I convince you to buy so much waste with some paper
that's killed off the trees, destroying your nature;
I pollute you with toxins, for which you pay money,
which then makes you laugh as your brain thinks it's
    funny.
My chemicals spread within earth and through skies,
which further allows me to tell you more lies.

I close your right hemisphere, your holistic feeling,
so the left brain then dominates, denying your healing.
Dead neurotransmitters, you act like a robot
that only makes money for a machine that's forgotten
the meaning of love.

Now we are all trapped, we've lost touch with our need
to be one living organism that finds joy in a song,
in a smile or a thought, or a simple kind deed.
Because of me, your words reflect the real you no longer.

RIDDLE OF THE MIND

I can manipulate you to see others with fear,
with jealousy, hatred or selfish behaviour.
Any pursuit of oneness has long been released
to desires for pleasure that deny you your peace.

I fill you with doubt and denial of your greatness,
so you suffer and hide from your true self and wait
while I allow you to feel all alone in this world,
cut you off from the bliss of the energy swirling
through the cells of your body and the joy that this
    brings.
I've convinced you you have no power to heal living
    things.

I disallow you to breathe consciously, you're frantically
    thinking,
which prevents you from feeling your energy sinking.
I create an imbalance that leads only to pain
unless you end this insane cycle and start breathing
    again.

But now you are trapped, no solution to find.
Have you worked out my riddle?
Yes, I am your mind.

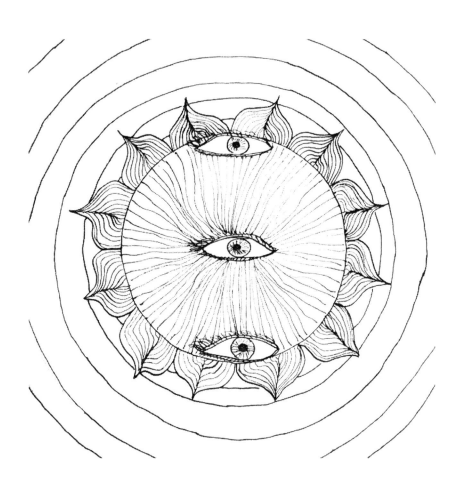

Sex-botic Nation

I did not know that we were all sex objects, being ogled at
    through lenses of perverse disguise,
or that a girl cannot look at her fellow sister without
    judgmental or dismissive eyes.
Is this really the world we want to live in, where our
    minds are conditioned to fantasise
and break a human body down into tiny parts, picking
    favourite bits to prioritise?
Through our diseased desires we seem to treat others in a
    delusional and discriminating fashion...

What happened to the passion?
Where soul meets soul and sees the other through a real
    connection,
feels the other's presence
and shares laughter and stories that reminisce of the
    bond of oneness
that runs through each and every one of us...
To look into the other's eyes and realise they are a true
    reflection
of your own real nature, and see them as perfection,
with unconditional love and unquestioning acceptance...
Or to come across a stranger and treat them as an equal,
using senses beyond the ego and know there can be joy in
    every conversation,

a chance for evolution, for laughter and for learning,
establishing friendship and actual human relations...
Or we can continue observing with an animal intention,
undressing one another with conditioned eye, mind
    drooling over their presence -
such blissful existence!

So when I smile at a passer-by, if he is not sexually
    attracted to me,
or if she views me based on physical appearance with
    negativity,
I'll get sneered or laughed at or perceived as if I'm crazy;
but it's fine by me as I smile knowingly, peacefully within,
yet bemused by the suffering so many choose to live in,
like mechanical machines unconsciously contributing
to society's goal of a robotic nation,
all sending signals of separation,
fearful in observation and denying our true colours of
    light and divinity...

...instead of living as one family: souls creating reality
through the perception of higher seeing,
floating through the space we breathe in,
harmonious in dance,
a magical hypnotic trance.
Only love to be giving and simultaneously receiving,
viewing people in the light of absolute
as water, earth, fire and air and spirit,
their consciousness, thoughts and perceptions,
no part of which belongs to any superficially judged
    identity,

with no regard to clothing, hair style, bust size or physique,
seeing past the societal concepts of beauty.
By observing another's inner light, we allow them to grow,
and by living naturally we allow our own hearts to glow;
we give a gift to Mother Earth, for she is conscious too
and realises we are one with her, just as I am one with
 you.

Music's Medicine

Feeling the beat take over me,
filling my body and mind with serenity
like a wave washing away all the impurities,
as music's melody sets my soul free.

From the moment the groove syncs with my heartbeat,
all negativity and worries disappear into the infinite sea,
and I realise I am nothing but a single drop amongst the
    waves;
yet without this drop the game of life would not be in play.

Music soulfully shows how connected I am,
helps me remember I am part of the divine plan;
I am a vibration of light and sound,
in tune and at one with the world around.

As I succumb completely to music's gift,
my spirit merges with the eternal abyss;
and in that moment I am completely free to be,
as time disappears into the timeless reality.

That moment of now being all that exists
as the sounds of surrender fill me with bliss.
The delusions my mind created drift effortlessly away,
leaving me floating to the melody with a smile on my face.

Just like the drop that spreads out on the surface,
being in harmonious dance allows other movers to calm
    the mind's race;
for when I am at ease to be me and dance freely,
this powerfully creates a ripple that affects those around
    me.

Spirit now swims through all of the channels
as we all succumb to our bodies' desires to flow through
    the waves and angles.
Mind, body and soul rhythmically at one
with life's freedom and heartbeat, in joyful song.

Alchemy Festival

I bounce up to Alchemy to see a multitude of colour,
yet unaware of the surprises in store for this rainbow
    warrior.
The campsite is cramped,
nature blesses me with my own patch of land,
a private hammock floating between the trees,
eagle-eye view for this nature-loving queen.

My true inner nature is instantly reflected
as I see a Buddha sand structure, beautifully formed.
Instinct pulls my wandering feet straight over to the
    crystals,
a dream reminding me of the surreal mystical
energy that connects every being here on Earth.
The lady stood in front of me - I met her once in dream
    world -
and in this dream I was her, wandering through a forest
    in the night
whilst crystal pyramids appeared everywhere,
no escape from the true path towards the light.
What I learned from this dream was really spectacular,
that we can never run away from our essence, our higher
    nature.
This waking life then brings me my very own crystal
    wand,

handed by the woman from the dream, showing that we
are all one.
The beauty of this crystal was that it represented my body
and chakras,
the pure kundalini light and the seven symbolic colours.
But the price was too high so the wand could not be
mine...

However, following events taught that we belonged
together,
throughout all space and time.
I offered a friend my hammock for free
so she gave me a fiver for my generosity,
which brought my grand total up to fifteen pounds.
Ten minutes later the dream lady came and placed the
wand in my hands...
Her higher self told her that I should have this crystal
for exactly fifteen pounds, with no rational explanation.
It's amazing what life can magic up when we're all on the
one harmonious sound.
Love is the strongest energy.
It seems that physical reality changed to help the crystal
and me unify for creativity.

Next, to a shaman's apothecary selling natural herbs from
around the world,
medicinal mushrooms, natural highs and herbal teas,
my eyes welled up from the genuine joy this brought to
me.
No need for police or unnecessary authority.
So many children of the Earth here, living as one free
community,

cosmic care providing shelter for those in need,
a safe haven with warmth and help, a place to feel at
   peace.
Strangers offering fresh chai tea,
lovingly made around a fire, with no request for money.

Lying beneath stars, a stranger brings me a blanket to
   help with the cold.
Through night's magic and glowing moon,
to sensational sunrise and a singing bird's tune;
a tribal style gathering with flames and drums,
jamming and chi-dancing, seeing hearts, having fun.
A surreal feel of energy and a real bond of unity,
ancient lights connected round a fire dancing
   rhythmically.
Natural energy and human power,
we have to pedal faster if we want the music louder!
Music heals our cells on the Liberty and Mushroom
   stages,
solar-powered by our unconditionally giving sun's rays.
Hula hoops left for all in the enchanted woods,
all day and night with no ownership or rules.
I am then blessed with healing while hands connect to
   Mother Earth's tree,
a haunting didgeridoo physically swirls my body, a
   penetratingly powerful energy.

In ancient times we are living,
unconditional love this festival was giving.
The truth of brotherhood, sisterhood and one,
essential for the living of life's eternal song.
Spirit and form played this game hand in hand,

working together in our magical homeland.
Be the change you wish to see,
we are the change that this world needs:
the illusions of separation and negativity
replaced by love and harmony.
Thank you, Alchemy.

Soul Sisters

Sisters of this Earth,
remember your divinity and your true worth.
Awaken your inner goddess,
reclaim your power and be honest
with your true heart's desire.
Allow the burning of the fire
that is deep within your psyche...

You are an independent creature of the night,
so allow the moon's magic to be your guide.
Raise the serpent energy that resides,
engage in activities and never compromise
the perfection that is your nature.

Be the healer and creator.
Be the friend and be the lover.
Be the compassionate, caring mother.
Show child and man how truly to accept,
with unconditional love, affection, joy and wit.
Be a role model of peace and take care of your soul.
Remember you are here to help this world...

You are a divine incarnation of the spirit of Mother Earth.
You are brave and selfless for choosing to incarnate as a
    girl,

for your pain runs deep just like the mighty tree's roots.
Memories of suffering are shared through the connection
of truth,
and the spirals of your subconscious bringing suffering
upon your youth.
Yet for this great sacrifice, eternal love is now given to
you...

So thank you, dear sister, for assisting with karmic
healing.
Remember always to remain true to your senses, intuition
and inner feeling,
no matter how false minds judge or wrongfully perceive
things.
Your intention is all that matters in the real world of
unity.
Realise your essence, share your truth and empower your
community.
Please, dear sister, brighten the world with your light.
Inspire hearts through your song... you truly are beauty
divine.

Shadow Surfacing

I was so blind.
How did I not see you?
So far to the one and the collective was my mind.
I knew you were a reflection;
all the love and beauty you showed me,
yet I failed to attach those qualities to you personally.

I finally understand what you meant by saying that we
    used each other.
For a long time I was hurt, confused,
I saw our journey as two souls helping one another see
    the light.
Now I see the other side of the story -
the dark and the light need to be fused.

When I saw tears roll down your beautiful face,
I thought you were hurting at how you may be affecting
    me;
yet now I see just how hurt you were by me,
for us to look into each other's eyes and for me genuinely
    not to care,
not show any anger, jealousy or painful despair.
We were once in love and she was my soul sister,
yet I only wished love and blessings upon you both;
the ultimate sacrifice necessary for the good of the whole.

No ego or signs of separation sent out,
just acceptance and love,
yet denial of the dark.

For years I was convinced it was wrong to make love,
due to repressed emotions
and a subconsciously suppressed, shadowy grudge.
Looking back, I see how heartless I must have seemed.
We were in love... we were two in one.
I still remember the drawings and poems I put my heart
    and soul into.
I'll never forget how you helped me, how we grew.
Do you not see that I equated my spiritual journey with
    you?

My reality was one of magic, eternity and divinity,
the one consciousness experiencing itself through duality.
A true god, a light being sent from above,
soul mates throughout all time and space;
yet the more I found oneness, the more detached I
    became.

I don't know why it had to be this way,
but obviously we had to go our separate ways;
I guess we grew apart on very different waves.
I was searching for my own truth and my own inner light;
now I fully realise what you meant by "Music is life."

You are my reflection, my love,
an aspect I refused to accept;
the darkness and the shadow self that I no longer shall
    reject.

For as soon as I accept the part of you that I chose not to
    see in me,
only then can I be the light and set my spirit free.

Thank you.

Twin Flame

I am so in love with your being.
When I'm around you, my core shakes and tingles with
    excitement.
My cells dance and come to life,
I feel energised and on a natural high.

I feel safe, comforted, at ease.
All that is me can just be... be free.
A complete reflection... beauty to perfection,
woman and man... we are the yin and the yang.

We are two existing as one,
floating rhythmically in harmony.
The energy I feel when we are alone
is a surreal sensation, feeling truly at home.

My being senses signals of wanting to flow closer to your
    inner being,
to hug you and to heal you... share your warmth.
The connection I feel, eternally deep and nothing more
    real,
cannot be explained - yet I shall try...

We are a pattern of particles that have been swimming
    throughout all ages,

the same wave in space and time,
twin flames of light, musically aligned,
communicating on a telepathic flow of time and mind.

We are one heart and soul,
one higher entity
avatared into two cells of knowledge, truth, love and
    power,
one consciousness existing as me and you.

No other soul could I ever desire;
sharing our dreams and fears lifts our spirit higher.
We share the magic and joys of life,
growing and learning together from the higher eye.

We could never judge, control, mistrust or act from ego.
When not around you I am content being alone,
for the time we spend together is blissful in every now.
My true love and a blessing, our love makes this world
    spin round.

We are ancient family members from the same tree,
longing for this world to unite in love, in peace, in
    harmony.
We know our mission and our purpose here, for spreading
    love and truth.
For everything my shared note of soul...
I humbly and eternally thank you.

Ancient Lovers

A majestic connection,
divine reflection,
friends and lovers,
comfort from just being around one another.

When their lips entwine,
the speakers sing softly in perfect time,
music's lullaby observing their sublime kiss,
true lovers breathing life into the other's lips.

When their bodies intertwine,
their hearts, souls and minds
combine, as one wave amongst the ocean,
one stream of consciousness in flowing motion.

Their bodies dance rhythmically, with synchronicity,
feeling a melding of each other's spiritual energy.
The one consciousness of heart and love
coursing through individual form in harmony.

They are the light... love...
the illusion...
the opposing poles of the law of confusion,
space and time unconditional in infinite fusion.

Love is the strongest vibration,
yet simultaneously an illusory distortion
allowing for the forever singing sounds of being,
without which separation there would be no life.

Her light offers his soul a helping hand.
His touch allows her to feel true love from a man.
They learn the balance required to be
god and goddess, creating a rhythmic sea.

The karmic cycle fascinates -
how the play of their dancing eyes
can turn the concept of dual masturbation
with all its modern negative connotations,
into an act of love, uniting the population.

For from the heart they inspire,
distancing themselves from animalistic desire,
the confusion of one being split into two,
yet choosing to live higher and move to spirit's tune.

They are ancient lovers succumbing to the will of Source,
raising the consciousness of the planet through healing in
    repetitive course.
Once more we have returned to a golden age of time,
natural forces working with gods and goddesses divine.
It is the light that connects these stars
that enables the sun and moon eternally to dance.

Perceived Point Of View

The point is always the same yet with different
    perspectives,
holographic directions, subjective and objective,
no right or wrong or good or bad. Just acceptance.
Intention being the discussed question,
questioning initiating the interplay between just being
and the conversation for perceiving.
Back and forth like a yo-yo words flow,
with moments of silence allowing the space for
    manifestation,
peace from mind, true connection.

The same answer given in two different ways...
the word now being verbalised, the experience of now
    being experienced.
The first moment of my life when someone asked the
    meaning of life,
and I could give an answer,
the answer being that precise moment,
no language necessary to describe what is occurring,
the senses and the snapshot self-explanatory,
points of existence continuously merging.

Polar opposites face to face,
a living, breathing, dying plant inbetween the space

and we feel its presence.
Two people yet a sense of three.
I break off a leaf -
that is not like me, yet it is what it is
and I do not judge my action.
From one point it is an act of compassion,
allowing the green more room to breathe;
yet from another perspective, there was no reason to hurt
    this breathing plant...
But as reasoning is misconceiving, why question it?
Accept it.

Now the picture within the picture, repetitively
    reproduced, has passed.
That meaningful, paradoxically pointless empty moment
    just a memory,
a scrics of cmotions and senses,
observations and perspectives.
Opinions reflect the individual reality,
yet combine to the one conscious entity.
Truths differ from person to person, sun to air, animal to
    greenery,
for every point of existence is pure consciousness,
aware of everything,
conscious of all proceedings.

Sizes and shapes of mind oscillate between realities,
worlds within worlds, between spaces of musical
    geometry,
feelings and senses giving form to the one formless
    reality...

PERCEIVED POINT OF VIEW

Such variety of words I could continue to use,
with no substance or truth for the feeling felt has now
    been abused
by the vast scale of semantics that language creates.
If seen as a burden, I understand now why some choose
    to feel hate
for this eternal game of characters the divine chooses to give.
We learn and relearn until there's no more to live.
This timeless trap of suffering we ourselves perpetuate
    with each breath...
As soon as we reach the light, like moths we begin to
    migrate
back to the darkness of self and of pain,
always aware we ourselves are to blame.
For the female and male go hand in hand,
with no separating if we're to stay in our homeland.

So I have, now, no choice but to accept life is suffering,
a goddess yet an ant marching through all the buffering
on a timeline of fear and love, with distortion ringing
    through each ear,
yet with the freedom that comes from acceptance and
    knowing.
Still only love to give, and this is what makes me lucky
for wherever I go I am blessed with beauty, shelter and
    smiles,
and somehow have enough money.
Now I realise that I can be surrounded by a sea of
    darkness, with tears rolling down my face,
yet my light will infinitely glow and shine joy to the world
    and human race.
This is how we accept...

This is how we live...

By seeing our own light and projecting and reflecting it.

By realising there is no right or wrong and only our
perception,

we can see the truth in others and give them
recognition.

So back to the beginning, where this wondering all
started.

Someone may be able to access all points of perspective
instantly,

question opinions in a heartbeat,

offer insight in ways incomprehensible to most human
minds

like a cosmic computer with intelligence exceeding all
space and time.

Yet is this really of any use if the being cannot feel any of
their beliefs,

ignorant of the concept of energy within every conscious
entity,

the point of mergence between us all?

Feeling only experienced by experiencing through
breathing,

believing in a feeling that can only be felt by believing,

combining the mind with body and spirit until achieving
higher seeing...

So having the dubious blessing of wisdom and quick
thinking

is suffering, unless coexisting with the feeling and the
healing.

We can become lost down the rabbit hole with nowhere to go

unless we accept every moment as perfection and go with
    life's flow;
breathing and silence are essential for the space in which
    to grow,
balance is required in order to remain in the show
that we call life.
A state of no mind can attain bliss within each one of us,
the heart being the door and love the key.

Whichever way round we say it,
freedom from thought will set us free.

Soul Seduction

The first time I encounter my reflection is through the
   music.
My fingers and bass guitar in harmonious action,
greeted by the tones of this soul's seductive saxophone.
A sexual sound and yet no physical attraction,
for the beauty I see symbolises his divinity,
the glistening gold and smooth flow from a hand's stroke,
the birth of sweet sounds in a musical meditation.
His face is at blissful ease whilst in simultaneous
   concentration,
one with my bass groove and our natural connection.

When the music stops and we converse through speech,
I realise he represents another aspect of me.
His life consists of a story, his story equates with my life,
and my higher mind sees that it is music's story,
the main theme being light.
As time goes on and we share life's song, I learn more and
   more,
teach and absorb,
change many of my set beliefs to questions,
understanding the entrapment of my mind's distractions.

This man tests me,
pushes my views of life to the extreme,

enabling me to experience the true meaning of duality.

Through the music we entwined and through the same
    sound we separate,

two aspects of the self to which we truly can relate.

Whilst I disagree with many of his views and see them as
    insanity,

it is the notes of our communication that construct our
    collective reality.

By offering new perspectives and sharing sounds that feel
    divine,

he soulfully seduces the workings of my mind.

A Journey Through Grace

This is a journey of Grace...
a story from the sounds of space
of the timeless time that moves apace...
Allow the words on the page to recreate the dream...
travel through the realms of mind, the unknown and
    unseen,
as you perceive her story through the mystery we call
    reality.

The feet that lead my body
hollow to the place where the peace within dwells,
dream to destiny, destiny to dream, inseparable.
The smile on the baby's face while her laughter sings over
    sentient souls discovering truth about the drops and
    the ocean:
*Big Questions by Little People, Answered by some Very Big
    People*
was the title that the smiling face read
of the book in which the story that was being told
played out within my head.
My path to re-awakening to the divine led me to what was
    already found,
the holy land...
Me. Within and around,
all sight and sound,

smell and touch,
slow wave and rush.

From another time my soul was here,
where I first learned that even death should have no
    fear.
Hovering in the middle of the ocean,
waves crashing over me, vessel spinning and circling in
    repetitive motion.
Although I did not know the storm was me, created by me
    and for me for our evolution,
I still embraced the unknown.
Yet now I know life and death are forever in fusion,
and this perfectly timed wheel has brought me back to
    Ton Sai,
my Thailand paradise, my holy illusion.

My favorite memory from last visit was the night before
    the storm,
and here I am in that same Small World bar,
with a golden ginger, furry creature comforting my
    wandering feet,
purring beauty breathing steadily to the rhythm of the
    jungle beat.
Three places since I first put pen to paper,
yet one stream of consciousness and constant heartbeat
writing these lyrics straight from the creator.

Meditating on a kayak in the middle of the ocean,
current dragging me away from land to increase my
    confusion;
I think I'm stuck.

Between island of green, in the middle of the sea,
fighting whatever destiny has chosen for me -
until I accept that I have no control and go with life's flow
for only then would fate allow my return to golden shore.
The message was clear:
only embracing love and being lost can conquer fear.
So now the storm is coming once more,
with Babylon's walls crumbling to the floor
enabling the opening of unopened doors;
the re-energising of my core is being allowed
by this timeless pattern of perfection
to perform.

Through all my travels I was searching for the love I could
    not find;
to believe that I could find it externally kept me suffering
    in denial.
I found happiness in all the beautiful beings and
    experiences of joy,
yet this elongated my journey to finding my true place in
    this world
and the peace within.
My reality starts from the inner levels of this skin,
the external being a reflection of the state of mind I'm in.

Now I am finally home,
for home is where the heart is and my heart is
    everywhere.
"Where is the mirror with the shells?" I hear an angel
    faintly whisper.
This perfect Om of one splits into drops on the same wave
    of mind and time to provide this next rhyme,

for the answer to what is sought shares my own trail of
   thought with the question asked by my fellow sister...
Reflection.
Beauty within is beauty around,
true perfection.
The colour of our revolving eye creating perception,
twisting all our journeys into one in this cycle of
   redemption.

Life is one of music and numbers,
Maths and emotion,
words and the unspoken.
For to search for the heart in this musical play of art,
space and time, form the arch that waves of connection
   allow us to hear;
with no sea there would be no ear and to listen we must
   truly hear.
In this infinite wheel of searching and learning,
we breathe in order to attain true nurturing
for without the air we would not see and where there is
   sight exists the one eye,
without colour, sound and silence, no eternal pi,
without the Earth, no form to conquer fear in.
Without the spirit, there is no space for senses to perceive
   what is real
in this twisting and turning reality,
magical, miraculous, yet with so much confusion.
As the words you are reading enable you to interpret
   differently,
with differing meanings, so the one feeling I'm
   conveying
is being lost to split signalling,

yet simultaneously remembered by the web of universally
    communicating:
you and me, sun and sea, air and tree,
Earth and divine art,
our heart.

And so back to the point I'm at in this magical crazy song,
written in the bar where I express my soul...
This really is a small world.

The Peace Within

The peace within...
All that is manifests from the state of mind we're in,
the external a reflection of the inner workings of the skin.
A Buddha nature yields a world free from sin,
as we powerfully produce through the energies of thought
    and action
a peaceful mind of unity and stillness, resulting in
    compassion.

Thus we affect the world around, with a gift of strong
    healing,
for remaining peaceful within allows for greater feeling;
a balance between body and mind, dissolution of hostility,
allowing spirit to flow freely and to heal the world's
    atrocities.
Inner conflicts only brings dis-ease on a collective scale,
the individual self-interest contributing to the whole.
The peace within...
The world around us is a reflection of the state of mind
    we're in.

Star Seed Secrets

What if we were autonomous sovereign beings, completely
connected to our world?
What if we were unconsciously enslaved by an alien race,
suppressing our souls?
What if the electromagnetic radiation of technology took
control and we didn't even know?
If our consciousness were hijacked by artificial
intelligence, could we ever truly grow?

What if computers, televisions and radio waves interfered
with our DNA?
What if electrical pollution affected the natural course of
evolution, damaging the neurons of our brains?
What if a global computer cut us off from our galactic origins
and this artificial intrusion is already the reason for all
our divisions?

What if we were really star seeds, who could transcend
this three-dimensional reality?
What if we were multi-dimensional beings capable of god-
like status, as described in mythology?
What if Atlantis is real, an archetype of Earth without
scientific dominion,
and it is being currently experienced by many, whilst the
majority remain blinded in submission?

What if Buddha, Jesus, Krishna, Moses, Mohamed and
    the other divines we admire
were humans who realised their cosmic origins, evolved
    higher and owned their true power?
What if the alien race who many believe are the ones
    entrapping our souls,
are the bankers, politicians and media moguls who stayed
    on our planet to impose their control?

What if someone were to break from the programme and
    escape this constructed version of reality?
If there were beings free of enslavement, how would they
    show their sovereignty?
Would they say governments use cunning methods to
    control our minds?
Would they suggest that they are from the future,
    volunteering to help mankind by returning to this
    timeline?
Would they claim that races such as the Arcturians,
    Pleiadians, Sirians, Lemurians, angels and the Galactic
    Federation of Light
exist and are actively helping humanity by sending signs
    and breaking through the walls of our imprisoned life?

What if these cosmic travellers told us all this, and then
    had the nerve to say
that they were the ones who created the technology to
    transmit truth through these waves?
If technology were intended to enslave, control and
    suppress our consciousness,
could it not also be directed to the exact reverse if those
    with love in their hearts took control of this global chess?

If scientific advancement were ultimately preventing
    natural evolution,
and this truth came directly from experience,
would you want this star seed to share the truth, or
    would you want me to keep it secret?

Dream Space Dreamers

Dream writing by a waking character,
consciously aware as a dream space avatar,
experiencing reality in the cosmic playground
and living out the dream through this holograph of sound.

Dream words for woken dreamers,
who'll never sleep again to the matrix deceivers,
always fully conscious of neurological receivers
transmitting and inputting with other light working
    believers.

Dream programmes for a cosmic radio,
the unconscious bringing forth ideas through which we all
    may flow.
While the ego plays along to the illusion of the show,
the dreamer sends out signals helping other dreamers grow.

Dream pictures of this formless universe,
where mind's creating matter just for fun, and to converse
with itself; for all that is is just the space,
so mind enjoys itself within the sleeping human race.

Dream parasites pollute this paradoxical sea,
yet without these sleeping viruses this recording could not
    be,

this sound submissively circling and at one with Source's
    dream,
which knows that love shall always reign and persists in
    the unseen.

Dream travelling through a timelessness conceived
as we teleport through the spaces in a world of make-
    believe,
existing simultaneously in parallel realities,
returning now and then to dream the light into vitality.

Dream rules governing the changes of the game,
but when we dreamers wake together life will never be the
    same;
for love will magnify when Source recognises itself in
    another me,
and another conscious dreamer within the dream will be
    set free.

Mother's Creation

Today, a baby's born.
He is surrounded by nurses, by doctors and medical care
as his family waits nervously outside, tension running
    through the air.
His mother lies exhausted, full of drugs and pumped with
    chemicals,
which now flow through this fragile body, undermining
    nature's miracle;
the father is full of joy as he looks into the innocent eyes,
yet he cannot possibly relate to his partner's emotions,
    even if he tries.
So this beautiful new soul senses signals of a divide -
sounds, sights and thoughts that from the moment of
    birth will forever now abide.
Yet if a picture were to be taken of this dynamic,
    interactive hospital scene,
everything appears to be in order, in the eyes of society.

Today, a baby's born.
Her mother's lying peacefully in a bath at home,
warm and gentle waters surrounding her and this new
    life's throne,
as a divine and beautiful, much loved little creature
travels a canal of light into a world of healing nature.
The father is full of joy as he looks into the innocent eyes,
dispelling any tension, waiting for the music of her cries.

The angels have been called and the baby's guides do all
　　they can
to assist the incarnation, part of the divine plan;
this girl is blessed eternally with love, with joy and
　　lightness,
she'll grow up one with nature and increase the Source's
　　brightness
in the world. Her mother appreciates the sacred essence
　　of the scene,
at ease with candles, soft music, crystals, and a body
　　that's drug-free.
A loving mother and father is all this new life sees,
sensing her first environment free of negativity.
The picture that's now taken from any observing mind's
　　eye
will make the trees to sing, the air to smile, and love to
　　travel far and high.

Today, a baby's born.
Years pass by as this lucky little life grows up carefree,
living in a huge mansion and surrounded with prosperity,
never having to worry about possessions, comfort, wealth
and always able to afford to pay for perfect health.
A queen surrounded by her toys, her nanny dresses her
　　and feeds
her with the best, ordered by her mother to provide for all
　　her needs;
this little angel seems to be the luckiest girl alive,
her excited mother's face lights up in smiles when she
　　arrives home.
This mother's dressed in beautiful and expensive designer
　　clothes

with perfect hair and face and body, she seems constantly
to glow;
women admire and men desire her, she commands the
attention of all within sight,
while her beautiful creation lies waiting for her affection,
crying alone each night...

Today, a baby's born.
The years are passing and another little life grows up
carefree,
stimulated mentally, emotionally, physically and
spiritually,
and always interacting with his loving family.
He has all he needs - love, affection, nature, laughter,
beauty,
education, learning and a sense of his security.
The toys he plays with and the clothes he wears
have all come from his brothers, with marks and tears,
yet in perfect condition that fulfills his every need,
there's no desire for surplus, no envy or greed.
This little angel appears to be the luckiest boy on Earth
as he lives, loves and learns in a family that knows his
worth.

Child's Play

Let us put ourselves into a child's mind:
no irrational worries or conditioned concept of time,
intuitively in tune with life's natural waves,
playing the game harmoniously with a smile on the face.

Let us live life with a child's observation,
inquisitively questioning and learning from reflection,
treating all they come across as a chance for information,
absorbing sounds and scenes to use for later life's creation.

Let us try and learn from the children's way of living,
innocent and caring with unconditional love from birth -
until we indoctrinate and disturb them with the signals
    we are giving
of anger and hostility that separate them from Mother
    Earth.

Let us travel to the inner workings of a child's mind,
no set beliefs or dogmas towards life to make them blind
to receiving cosmic symbols, archetypes and ideas,
open to the collective consciousness with universally
    connected ears.

Let us use a child's growing fingers in our touch,
let us have adventures, climbing trees and suchlike,

looking lovingly into a petal and seeing its timeless
    beauty,
gazing at a stream, surrendering to simplicity.

Let us find a rock and play with it for hours,
believe in magic, endless joy, and find healing from plants
    and flowers;
let the sky be our medicine and the stars be our teachers,
asking the sea for answers as if the waves were our
    mind's speakers.
Let us, without embarrassment, dance when we hear a
    song,
letting all inhibitions go, not caring if we are dancing
    'wrong'
but listen to our bodies and allow our senses to be in flow,
without fear of being judged, allowing the inner child to
    grow.

Once Upon A Time

Once upon a time we lived in a world of war craft,
we would send our brothers off to die for power, oil and
land.
We would raise an innocent soul from birth to be
brainwashed by society's say-so,
to make money for a robotic system that had forgotten the
humane way to behave.

We were made to believe that human nature is selfish,
nasty, brutish and short;
we were convinced that there were not enough resources
to share, resulting in insanity and war
when we would rape our women, even our children, for a
pleasure that could never be satisfied
with no compassion or remorse for the pain we would
cause. So much suffering for a brief, primal pastime.

We would torture and kill with no intention or will, simply
because the ego took control.
Lost from our path, many would even laugh at the
atrocities committed all around the world.
We would cut down our trees as if we were a parasite, a
cancer spreading over the globe
and we were responsible for the death of countless species
by continuously destroying their homes.

We polluted our skies and water supplies, which
    eventually led to the breakdown of health.
Just like a disease, we dumped chemicals in our seas,
    which led to decreased food production.
We would force our children to work and live in horrific
    places and conditions,
with no education or learning, no real love, just yearning
    for a life denied by submission.
We allowed them to suffer unloved and alone until many
    died of starvation,
while the rich over-ate, wasting endless food that our
    Earth had supplied for all nations.

We implemented a plan for population control so the
    ones with money and power could remain in
    charge.
We consciously created illness and disease, allowing fear
    and death to spread fast and far.
We poisoned the food and told lies to our youth, allowing
    global oppression.
We were brainwashed and our intelligence diminished,
    like slaves with no powers of action.

We altered our own neurons and cellular DNA with
    electrical radiation from technology.
We handed over our minds and sacrificed our hearts for a
    global monopoly
of corporations that ruled with no morality or care for the
    nature that sustained
all life on our Earth; this destroyed our true worth, as
    pursuit for money dominated the brain.

Actions became desperate, dominance and injustices
    amplified in severity.
New ideas were introduced and governments increasingly
    pursued the battle to remain in sovereignty.

Yet no matter how hard they tried and with no reasons as
    to why, this disease failed to murder us all,
as the spirit of the Earth was eternally strong. So the
    trees regained natural rule.
Despite all the suffering, pain and hurt we caused to our
    planet, to fellow humans and the unseen unconscious,
from the beginning it was forgiven, love unconditionally
    giving, as it was all just a glimpse in a dream.
This construction of war on our Earth, this rape of roots
    and dominion of mind,
are all a memory of the psyche from a dark perspective of
    life
that happened once upon a time.

A Mermaid's Tale

I loved the feeling of my tail,
the way it always left a trail
of ripples, with the encompassing waves
upon my body with the cold I'd craved.
The sounds of movement circling around,
so many sensations simultaneously found
through one breath and one swim,
one vast ocean allowing me in.
My sea... my home...
permitted by the gods to be free to roam.

They're entrancing creatures, yet so strange;
how they can breathe in the air and not harm their
    brains?
How they can survive above water and only appear
once or twice in a lifetime, every one thousandth year?
The scriptures say they are aliens, creatures alone,
beings so mysterious that they do not wish to be known;
they are the sky gods, from another time and space,
sent here to show us that we are not the only race.

I wished to know more about these magical masters,
these transcendental alchemists that survive through
    disaster.
I once read an article that told of the story

when their world above was taken out with rage and fury;
their homes were destroyed, few survived left to weep,
yet still they remain, at peace in the deep.
And through cycles of time, generations have come and go,
yet why they associate with us, we can never truly know.

Then once I had the honour to meet one of their middle
    young;
at the seventh cycle of the light rising when my powers
    had just begun.
The elders' conch had been blown and the first drum beat,
a most magnificent pearl had been given, forever mine to
    keep.
The celebratory ceremony drifted by in a daze...
one moment I was mortal me, then by magic my DNA
    changed!
It was like I'd been sleeping for such a long time,
I could feel trickles of crystalline fluid drip slowly down
    my spine,
my vision intensified as I saw the world real, and
my tail glowed bright, I could feel each grain of sand.

Can you imagine what it's like *to feel each grain of sand?*
Or to smell the essence of something from far away, and
to hear each individual sound as if emanating from my
    brain,
memories once out of focus coming flooding back again.
I could tune into the timelessness of all my past reality,
somehow through the mystical waves that connected me
    to my family,
hear their thoughts, feel their feelings, see through all old
    illusions

and it all made sense in that moment of fusion -
why secrets had to be kept, in order for our race to be
(we're a magical race, my father once told me).
Yet how we compared to these gods of the sea
was still beyond my psychic ability.

That day I was blessed to meet this young one,
a deep desire came upon me to sing him my soul song,
it filled me entirely as I was too mesmerised to tell him,
so I sung from my heart and could feel his every cell
merge with my spirit, as we danced with one energy,
entwined through the air, feeling hypnotised to be
completely at ease and at one with this frequency.

As the music grew louder my hands reached for his soul:
I knew I could heal him, give a gift from my world,
filling him with unconditional love. As I started
a glowing light flew from my hand to his heart
and in that moment I knew he was filled with bliss,
his eyes shining brighter than any orb I bore witness to.
His lips surrendered to a smile as I moved around,
and I could feel his whole being shake from my radiating
    sound;
colours danced within him and his breath sank over us,
and in that moment of ecstasy, he was overcome by lust.

My soul song stopped short and the orb washed away,
and the once enlightened look on this god's face
sank into despair as his heartbeat slowed
and his body became distant and cold.
Every part of him melted, merging into the abyss
as the gift of love and realisation of eternal bliss

now deserted this creature, his body lifeless...
But wait...
If my healing gift of pure light had caused his decease,
does that mean these men are mere mortals
and the true gods remain in the seas?

Galactic Time Traveller

Life turns into rhyme when broken from the cycle of time,
allowing us to raise our awareness and set a new
   frequency
for the human race.
Living in a multi-dimensional reality,
we realise our deep connection with the stars and other
   galaxies
and travel further into realms unseen.

Miraculous healings that were once deemed fiction now occur
as our abilities expand
together with our consciousness of universal supply,
allowing us physically to change neurology.
Our eyes see pure light and the aura glows with energy.

We can easily store information,
whether it be songs or visualisation,
written words or conversations.

When living as eternal beings, the music never stops...
We are always swimming and soulfully singing
through a current felt as infinite love.
For love is all there truly is.
We let go our old perception, based on mind's false
   subjection,
of separation.

For the soul is eternal and one with the external,
so when in tune with the universal music that surrounds
we see time's cycle disappear and everything existing as
    one sound.

We feel alive, always, and energised in the extreme,
ears listening to one frequency
with infinite possibility.
Telepathy and channelling, and distant place-time
    travelling,
now map the mind in re-creation
of knowledge and thought-form manifestation.
Psychic ability, endless holographic memory,
and even the power of invisibility,
are the tools of purest consciousness
when everything is just awareness.

Tunes are playing frequently through body, mind and soul,
and sensed fully and instantly
for we are the music's notes.
And within the silences, free of all desire, the higher mind
reminds us we are loved, powerful and appreciated,
comforted with loving words in rhyme.

Yet it's not just the sounds that hypnotise but the colours
    and the imagery.
We see the life force and feel its presence,
realise it is not separate for we are the energy.
Made in God's image,
the id and ego walk together hand in hand;
for living in the now and not the past or future
allows us to be the divine Man.

The Gift Is Life Itself

You want more, yet what can measure up to such a gift?
The very breath that gives you life,
the vessel that holds that breath.
Are you not in awe of its magnificence?
You are asked again,
are you not in awe of its magnificence?
Stop for a moment.
Now, breathe in and slowly expel that life force as you
    are asked,
what if it were taken away?
Would you beg for its return?
Would you value it then?

Sound Synapse

This astrologic-numerologic-philosophical use of words
creates a spiritually stimulating experience, enhancing
    verse as it is heard,
for the writing of a confusingly conscious, clever change of
    rhyme
produces poetry that reveals performance as
    unconsciously past its time.

But if we slow it down, we see that each word can be
    counted into line
as the chaos of our thought creates an order we perceive
    as rhyme.
In fact, the complex compilation of this neurologically
    interactive grand design
is just the fantasy that sound creates when structured by
    the mind.

Formless and nonsensical syllables serve no purpose but
    to rationalise
this perfect pattern of perpetual noise, creating a puzzle
    in binary disguise;
and as we wander through the endless maze of non-
    existent surprise
we see the ones that form the zeros and from the zeros
    come the eyes.

But the eye perceives, deceives and believes only what it
    misguidedly retrieves,
receiving information through senses subject to
    personality;
for the self shapes and relates all to its individually
    induced reality,
succumbing to the spell of an order that is in fact
    insanity.

The whole universe is mental, literally and
    metaphorically;
when we see the truth (and these words are proof) it all
    comes down to astronomy.
The choice of vowels and sounds spins round in an
    unconsciously spiralling vortex of space,
as astrologic-alliterations and numero-rhythmic
    vibrations flow through the formless thoughts of Grace.

If You Have Enjoyed This Book...

Local Legend is committed to publishing the very best spiritual writing, both fiction and non-fiction. You might also enjoy:

ONE PAIR OF SHOES
Mollie Peace (ISBN 978-1-907203-39-8)

Mollie Peace was one of a generation that saw the most extraordinary changes. Born in poverty, she lived through the hardship (and some joys) of the early twentieth century, experienced the tragedies of war and witnessed the birth of the motor car and the Internet. To have experienced all this while caring for her family and others in need was no ordinary life. Yet throughout, like so many other women of her time, she nurtured a private desire that was always denied her. She wanted to be a writer. That was her real identity. But there was no opportunity. Until now. These are her poems and short comic stories. "This collection of work is, quite simply, beautiful." *The Wishing Shelf Book Awards.*

AURA CHILD
A I Kaymen (ISBN 978-1-907203-71-8)

One of the most astonishing books ever written, telling the true story of a genuine Indigo child. Genevieve grew up in a normal London family but from an early age realised that she had very special spiritual and psychic gifts. She saw the energy fields around living things, read people's thoughts and even found herself slipping through time, able to converse with the spirits of those who had lived in her neighbourhood. This is an uplifting and inspiring book for what it tells us about the nature of our minds.

A SINGLE PETAL
Oliver Eade (ISBN 978-1-907203-42-8)

Winner of the national Local Legend *Spiritual Writing Competition* in 2012, this page-turner is a novel of murder, politics and passion set in ancient China. Yet its themes of loyalty, commitment and deep personal love are every bit as relevant for us today as they were in past times. The author is an expert on Chinese culture and history, and his debut adult novel deserves to become a classic.

SPINACH SOUP FOR THE WALLS
Lynne Harkes (ISBN 978-1-907203-46-6)

Gold Medal winner in the national *Wishing Shelf Book Awards*, this is a message of hope for anyone in despair. When we see our troubles as opportunities for growth, we can turn our lives around and "recognise the remarkable in the ordinary". Lynne has lived in many wonderful and colourful places, from South America to the jungle of Gabon in West Africa, and she describes graphically the resilience of the native peoples and the magnificence of the natural world. Yet she found herself retreating into unhappiness and isolation. This beautifully written book is the story of how she fought to rediscover her own spirituality and find a new way of thinking.

RAINBOW CHILD
S L Coyne (ISBN 978-1-907203-92-3)

Beautifully written in language that is alternately lyrical and childlike, this is the story of young Rebekah and the people she discovers as her family settles in a new town far from their familiar home. As dark family secrets begin to unravel, her life takes many turns both delightful and terrifying as the story builds to a tragic and breathless climax that just keeps on going. This book shows us how we look at others who are 'different'. Through the eyes of Rebekah, writing equally with passion and humour, we see the truth of human nature...

5P1R1T R3V3L4T10N5
Nigel Peace (ISBN 978-1-907203-14-5)

With descriptions of more than a hundred proven prophetic dreams and many more everyday synchronicities, the author shows us that, without doubt, we can know the future and that everyone can receive genuine spiritual guidance for our lives' challenges. World-renowned biologist Dr Rupert Sheldrake has endorsed this book as "...vivid and fascinating... pioneering research..." and it was national runner-up in *The People's Book Prize* awards.

These titles are all available as paperbacks and eBooks.
Further details and extracts of these and many
other beautiful books may be seen at

www.local-legend.co.uk

Lightning Source UK Ltd.
Milton Keynes UK
UKOW01f0352131115

262573UK00008B/149/P